THE GIFT OF SCREWS

Also by Brian Chan

Thief with Leaf
Fabula Rasa
Scratches on the Air (forthcoming)

BRIAN CHAN

THE GIFT OF SCREWS

PEEPAL TREE

First published in Great Britain in 2008
Peepal Tree Press Ltd
17 King's Avenue
Leeds LS6 1QS
UK

ISBN 13:9781845230050

 Peepal Tree gratefully acknowledges Arts Council support

CONTENTS

Two: Moth Glow

Three: Dive Song

Four: Cave Love

Five: Snow Moon

for Molly and Janice

The attar from the rose
Is not expressed by suns alone,
It is the gift of screws.

— Emily Dickinson

Одне:
NADA ANEW

WHEN NOTHING MOVES

                              the pen at the top
of an empty page, think of a book
with no author, imagine the sun
without its winds, yeast soaked in water
in kitchens with windows and doors shut,
    houses whose floors are unscuffed by any dance.

Out of such crumpled silence words still
climb, frozen loaves out of the basement
where deaf women yet dance with blind men
who sometimes pause to absorb the voice
of the wind by which nothing escapes
    being read and written, revised or erased.

So on Sunday sidewalks spread your texts
of twice-baked bread and still-rising dough.
All is given to be handed on.
This is the common good most ignore,
wealth of the bin that can't be emptied,
    that overflows as long as no tally's made.

ORACLE

If you feel this chart a blank slate,
know that it has been prepared for us
to draw the moment of our mind on.

Should it seem a near-empty bowl,
know that it is designed not to leak
a single drop of your molten gold.

And if you find it floats in a free state,
know that every border has been crossed
and every tribe challenged so that we might

begin to map our memory beyond
any nostalgia for one mother-
tongue or other investment of cowards.

TRANSCENDENCE

The useless matters: the invisible
waiting to be seen by eyes made again
naked as a newborn's: a bridge across
an open space that needs to remain
open: a domain without a border:

CHRISTINA GARBO

The pull of the pulse of a queen
surrendering her crown to transcend
the suffocating borders of duty

leads her across an abstract sea
whose rhythm is that of an endless
dying breath without hope of any heaven:

this is how humans once gods live,
beyond the moats of the routine claims
by lives of hellish ordinariness.

Now her final promise, of love,
has died, she imagines new desti-
nations, worlds in which the one freedom left

is to kiss the breath of life back
into a child choked by the bright songs
of the sea's careless obsessive sirens.

POWER (A SISTER'S DREAM)
    — for Sheril Woolgar

at night may I roam/against the winds... when the owl is hooting
at dawn may I roam / against the winds... when the crow is calling.
                                    — Sioux Dreamsong (trans. Densmore)

Christina, we drove through our desert until
we came to a gas-stop on Indian terrain.
You ignored the young attendant till he said
we had been driving with two tires near-flat
and you stalked off to find the nearest mirror
to powder your latest disappointment at.

Waiting for the car to be fixed, I sunbathed
with the young man in a pool behind the store.
We talked naked about everything we felt
we knew of the full wind-speaking tree nearby.
Like a cat he spoke, a gentle man whose eyes
flashed suns piercing and melting my spreading clouds.

To each other we would die, and to some thing
that could never, and, feeling only our hands,
lips and eyes open, I forgot about you.
On the road wheels knifed by, each driver driven
into believing he had somewhere to get
before the light drained out of the evening sky.

On a hill at the reddening horizon,
around a fire sat a group of Elders
like embers floating above an egg's shadow.
I heard them calling us to a kind of home
with its promise of the blending of all coals
into one flame as strong as each coal's dying.

Meanwhile were you dying somewhere else apart
from us witnessing the sparking of the stars,
the smoke of music rising behind the hill
as the Elders at our approaching dispersed
to leave us young people to our song and dance
of meeting and mating towards a new sun.

The next morning without you I drove away,
my latest death beside me where once you sat.
It is too late, my sister, under that tree
whose voice you cannot yet hear, to miss you locked
in your eternal pause of awaiting your
ideal death to lift you into heaven knows where.

TO ENTER

          another town, to wear
another tongue, to hear a strange flute
and to know all their rhythm before
their speech, their song, the familiar and
the new, and not to mind that sometimes
it's all a stony racket, a clash
of rocks the sea will make smooth, of knife-
blades which will sharpen one another
into profiles human of the moon.

EVENING DROWNED IN A DRY SWAMP

The flat quarrel of frogs belching between gulps
    of rain slapped down by a sky the very mother
of indifference, an unerasable grey,
    or the silver snoring of the six-o'clock bee
under the brittle drilling of deaf crickets
    forging twilight's soft breast into an armour-plate
against the neverending hammering curse
    of dogs beaten hollow between rooftops of tin
pelting their bricks of rage to have them hover
    in the mind's sky like clouds of blank slate or leaden
farts of thunder heard but not heard as having
    to be heard like the growls snarls yelps of beaten numb
men caught writhing in cobwebs of dumb memory,
    in nets of radio-prattle or in tight cages
of lashing song and dance fuelled by drumming
    veins swollen with thudding rum, the beat of hearts pumped
by the urge to dare, by aspirins of accept.

COMPENSATION

You here are so loath to even start
meaning anything that I wonder
if such reluctance is what forced art

to dissipate itself in revolt
against silence, like a thunderbolt
that folds down in backwards somersault,

or a craven prince, in the looming
shadow of an aloof king, forging
virtue out of violent silence.

So the legacy of Englishness
and its weapon of the left-unsaid:
colonies abandoned to a mess

of incestuous whispers and stammered
tributes to indifferent ghosts by numb
men pretending hard they're not only

consoling themselves with a vengeance.

TO A FISH OUT OF WATER

You know your loneliness is final
when the best words no longer comfort
and breath flows neither bitter nor sweet
in your indifference of a desert
whose cathedrals that match your cool are
looming around you like dried cacti.
Your despair rhymes with their stark stare but their
plainness finds no echo in your skew eye.

L'ANGOISSE DE LA PRAIRIE

I: *Wound*

The jagged bricks that pass for language stab
at the glass of my ears. This pain, only
        mine, is not mine only: not
        myself only, I cry out,
    a bird alive plucked, a child with no
    angel's feathers to mask its raw fire.

II: *Barrier*

Nurse, I've further split my tongue by spelling
the me of you, the you of me, and you
        reach over the flattened white
        of your breast only to drain
    the wound of its oil so as to wrap
    your dry gauze of words about its flame.

III: *Scarecrow*

In my field of trespass, black-and-white birds
mock my rainbow absence with thorns of tongue
        not rooted deep in any.
        At once clouds sprout beaks and teeth;
    and the wind's scythe slashes a dark scar
    through screams of grass and these witness eyes.

IV: *Sketch*

Not only the sky and wind but nothing
can be drawn save this becoming, something
        always only beginning
        to know itself. The rest is
    the grotesques of a blind man switching
    on and off his face his own hand's light.

THE BLIND SAMARITAN

Any light left to her house may be found
in its toilet where the lamp is blackened
as are her books to shit by, crammed tight
on shelves designed for holding headache-pills.

And she, social worker, something to do,
more loot, she of the tilt of head with eyes
of black diamond, dull mirrors, announces
the books shed light only on those who have
no hope of acquiring lawns and such
after eternities of torture and such.

Lady, just outside on your too-green lawn
your son's screaming at his crucified kite
scrawling a staggered ladder down past the sun
which the ripe fruit of the easter-tree makes black.

BLACK COFFEE IN A WHITE CAFE

In this bright day full
        of emptiness, all words fall
like screaming birds shot
by hungerless men.

Through that rain of corpses,
        I see you at the open door about
to cross the rug bridging
your dream and mine. Two dreams

are always crossing and some-
        times their authors know how not to let
the chance of a third, even
as it appears, fade. But white

fences are no less effective
        for being almost erased by the sun,
for the more children play behind
them, the tighter their
                        gates stay shut.

FOUR POEMS FOR LINDSAY WOOLGAR

I: CHILD, TREE, SLAVE

Between your sharp innocence and this business
called The World, between your need to dance and its
compulsion to whip itself into a craze
   of something called Work, stands the growing
simplicity of a sapling already
pruned towards a determined shape and encaged
by an unshifting mesh wrought from words of tin.

II: CHILDREN

Immigrants from the other side
of birth, heirs to native strangeness,
geniuses who learn foreign tongues
long before they're taught how to spell,
who begin unafraid to change
their accents from universal
madaba to parochial
brogue: speech their human destiny,
babble its stamp of density,
and dictionaries and grammars and
The Daily News its police.

III: AN EAST-INDIAN WEST-CANADIAN FAMILY

Sunday morning, long before the rest of the street can wake,
they're spilling out of their home, first the children, young and old,
playing with one another on their bikes, their voices bright
and clear without being raucous (but I don't sleep next door).

Grandfather steps out and checks out the sun, the plants, the kids;
his wife emerges and they start out on a walk, smiling,
glad to be still alive, safe, and passing on the blessing
with a touch to the heads of children who acknowledge them.

The children run to greet the yellow car their father drives
home on a break from his first shift and they fuss about him.
The youngest rides off and Dad claps a warning: Not too far!,
before going in to see his wife and to grab a Coke.

He comes back out, talks to the kids, then drives off, no hurry.
Bye Dad! in more than one language: it's a talent they have,
or a chance they don't resist. However hard their lives,
whatever new problems in this dry bald suburb of breath,

they keep hardship in its place as just one more chance to breathe
and, underneath it all, they know all their lives are one web
of interlocked spreading circles: a genius they still have
(and they'd dismiss you as odd if you tried to mention it).

IV: TRIBAL

At their barbecue-grill, man and woman joke
   I wasn't hungry before I smelt that smoke!
with heads bowed as though in prayer
   You think it's rare enough, dear?
before an altar contemplating
   I'm sure getting tired of waiting!
the promise of this latest fiction bridging
   These mosquitoes are greedy: my neck's itching.
their two plump minds into one dream of hunger.
   Right! Let's eat: we're not getting any younger!

VIEW FROM THE OTHER TOWER
  – for Sheril Woolgar

We looked up from our splintering pale faces
    and saw a ruined two-towered castle
    in which we would hide from the lion we
    had never seen and from the tribe we could
see approaching, dark and speared, to seize our pool.

In that tower we huddled, our tribe, for days
    until, all danger be damned, we pulled out
    our raw hamburger and fried it despite
    the giveaway smoke: who does not prefer
being eaten to being trapped or ignored?

When the quiet brutes arrived, they drank and washed,
    just like us civilised apes, except they
    seemed to fear neither lion nor castle
    nor our hiding in it: they were patient:
sooner or later we would have to come out.

For one, we women needed to wash our quims
    and the one safe way to reach the water
    was as gods to charm our way into it.
    So with round hymns we made our tower move
to the edge of the pool, and there we stepped down.

And, while our men sweated protecting the keep,
    we bathed once again in the waterhole,
    this time under the eyes of lion-men
    attending us in a way that made us
solider than stone and wispier than clouds.

Back fresh inside the tower, we smelt our boys
   were itching to repeat our trick, but they
   could not recall a single sacred song,
    so I knew their descent would spark a war.
Which tribe won't choose death over living as gods?

ANGELS

       fall off their clouds
of care to become fools
who walk tightropes and fall
off cliffs only to learn
how to turn into safe
burghers who step sideways,
around and back or not
at all, till they fall off
their rugs of calm to turn
shocked back into angels.

QUICK SCRAWL FROM TAHITI

There never was anything but the sea,
the newborn sky, and cliffs carved by time's wind.
That one man at the edge might still wonder
about it all and fool himself he means
something like why or anything at all,
while the rest of the tribe is out getting
on with filling up the day in the same
unquestioning way that has always kept
them warmed-up, is not the start of any
meaning to the indifference of the waves
but merely the mark of a dunce trying
to preserve his footprints on a wet beach.

Yet such nonsense hardens into meaning
and our statues are built accordingly.

— Putting down the postcard from which the man
has been erased, she claps her hands and sighs:
She'd love to be there lying in a chair,
soaking in the air and plotting next year!
For her that would be the whole of Just-So:
she is content with so little, so much
of no question, questions being always
only just born, too weak for sensation,
the fruit and food of a world of What-Next
set in unchallenged grooves too old to fade,
all things frigging themselves into Repeat,
despite the dictatorship of The New
whose trivia flash like bombs — because they can,
so-called Evil the flower of Why-Not.

NEED

Am I only part of an age, or am I all
     of each day, not of only
its blaring sadness? And if that sadness is just
     a slow stray train rattling through
the dark tunnel of one man melting at the core

of winter, can I expect you to complain with me
     that the train is too cold, too dark,
too slow in an age when everything can be measured
     and so ignored, even brothers
and sisters paid to explode in zones of death catered

by blue-suited criminals drinking champagne in rented
    hotel-rooms showing off the latest
models of weapons of mass-murder and such, guns and bombs
    designed by anonymous fingers
and assembled in factories by those they're designed to kill?

'I've no idea what a *man* is: all that I know is his *price*.'
    In an age of such casual madness, what
can it matter if our train's cold dark or slow, entering each
    tunnel like a rat through a hole that leads
to a trap? So we doubt, in the cage of an age that we think

final when it's only by fools fashioned, mechanics of the great
    forgetting by the numbing drug of dull words
like newspaper-bars against the streaming light of day that is ours
    to transform into as many miracles
as urged by desire that, train or no train, would read itself anew.

ATTENTION

The sheer everydayness of our miracles
outweighs the nonesuch of the ordinary
in moments like these of waiting without want
for the return of vision. If people will,
in hard plastic baskets, lug babies about
like eggs, and not like books, can they ever be
ready for the hard question of a spilt child?

BLOOD SPILT

Its misplaced purity terrifies:
    we fear for it as for a child tilted
        at the edge of a busy street: in having

to see it lies the pain. We prefer
    it hidden, contained to its safe circuit
        of Well, of course, let those accidents happen

to others, and TV tidy up
    broken limbs or hearts, pass the ketchup please:
        the real thing had better mind its own business

of not reminding us that time is
    running out as well as round and round and
        up and down the gasping ladders of our spines'

borrowed breath furnacing up our day's
    impatient pauses.

TURNING A CORNER

                        of his routine
busyness, to realise its fuel
is sadness leaving a trail of white smoke
behind him who must then pretend there is
nothing in his wake, an empty now
of loud silence being all he has left
in a world of blind ghosts dodging
one another and themselves voiceless
through their signals of choked sobs.

NO GHOST

        like the ghost of what might have been,
for it is a lonely monster, without
the fruit or fire of what is, the doors
of which it keeps knocking on for entry
to get itself mercifully murdered out
of its tormented limbo of an ideal
by the very mushroom god that spored it,
a god haunted by the fear that he has
never truly lived, even while searching
all over the clouds for signs of real life.
Maybe such adventure was a coward's
dodging of one moment that kept returning
to challenge him with its chances of real
power, its temptations of grand nothings
and, in between, its demands of stone choice
out of his quarry of dense indecision,
his ossified layers of postponement
– not of action, but of consciousness,
not of feeling, but of feeling's inclusion
of its shadow-twin into its blinkered
tyrant's domain of arrogance that passed
for awareness as it strode across the ruins
of Paris and Athens and Rome, while back home
the ghost thickened into a mist of pause
that prevented his house from being turned
into flats that would in turn be haunted
by rehearsals of tomorrow's remorse
for lives lived in full lust but without heart.

TO A GHOST

After you killed yourself your best
friends and strangers alike said
He was always a strange one...

I this Spring morning feel strange
walking into a sun strained
by a net of attendant clouds

holding their breath as they wait
for their king to breathe his last
so that they too might disappear

from above that line of machines
drilling holes from lawn to lawn
of homes with windows empty

of curious eyes: there is no
wondering why in this camp-
ground of convenient rape.

Is this why I left one tribe
behind, only this other
maze of murdering streets to feed?

I know you're one of those clouds
starting to leak through my eyes
as they surrender to the sun

they were not trying to stifle
but to filter and translate
into as many rainbows

as a stranger might need to help
him bear the claws of one more
crab of doubt climbing his spine.

LAKE

Not day's rabid vacancy
but the scope of its silence
cries out for another voice
that children playing strangely
quiet at water's edge may

embody like a cocoon
or that may already be
the fat blue tongue of the dog
tethered like a bored lion
ambling in an open cage

or the drawl of its owner,
a woman about to row
a quick boat out to its point
of anchor, there to await
her lover's separate craft;

or does that voice start to seep
through your sharp tones – each equal
to the next in its brightness
signalling safe tribal sense
as you help her man the boat

in return for a free ride –
leak as between the taut strings
of a harp stung by pebbles
pelted by a wind itself
flung in and out of being?

Or it may be none of these,
and instead the cry of men
searching for a boy gone lost
in an indifferent forest
or down the lake's cold wisdom.

CRAB

You can try to say anything
but beside the lapping water
eroding every pebble dreaming utterance,
anything said can mean anything else
and nothing can mean anything at all.

NADA

I give up one loneliness to another
when I admit that nothing means anything.

I no longer have to fool myself I
should try to touch or move you with my words
and can get on with my real work of breathing.

Words are mushrooms of fire and air and not
the rooted wings this mudcrab once needed
to believe in, and only in always
brimming silence can he begin to hear
the echoes of this ancient nada anew.

Two:
MOTH GLOW

RECOGNITIONS

Scraps of the soul drifting over the river of my eye,
    each on his or her angled way of essential
        forgetting of the threads linking us all,
            shred my heart into sparks of fear

and of joy that leap with the finding and fade with the loss
    of links frayed by the tension of seeing too well,
        the impulse of recognition staggered
            by a relentless remembering

both the finest stitch and the most ruthless unravelling
    of a quilt still spreading, impossible to check,
        whose patches of light are too brief to be
            held and too sharp to be ignored.

IN A CROWD

About me masks with holes for eyes, holes that don't want
to be charted or bridged, that have accepted all
    is a sucking abyss.

Already in the buds of young faces crossing
roads of Saturday night, the worm of obedience
    smears its red and green scars.

Faces like lanterns held dim above shoulders bent
already with old pain: backpacks of promises
    thin as the shells of snails.

While a smile glimmers still in the lanterns' eyes, cracks
of sadness have started to mesh beauty's soft glass
    with lines of submission.

As the firm fruit of youth races to such ripeness,
my seeding eyes resist the leaden yawn that tempts
    a tired heart to sleep,

sleep I deny in these attempts at meeting you
in your eyes, other of myself, you who would dodge
    the self that contains all,

all on different stages of the fiction of flesh,
the flags of flesh we wave to one another, bridg-
    ing chasms between spills

of identity, tags of separateness, words
of lonely projections, of crowded assumptions
    transcended by only

the humbling world-tongue kiss of jazz stretching the flat
and sharp edges of dividing speech into smooth
    spheres of embraceable

yous, familiar strangers greeting with eye and hand-
shake of love and desire, of mystery and memory,
    of promise *and* return.

DREAM

As I travel alone on crowded streets
the moon pulls my blood to its gates of tears
and I yearn to turn a corner and bounce
into the chance of your smile and the kiss
of your eyes, seeing us walk together
eagerly though we have nowhere to go
but beside within and through each other,
our hands knowing exactly what to say

when words can only fail a flooded heart,
while all about us the flutter of night
is the bright flag of an unflagging joy
and our every step a sure patient root
spreading upwards into a burst of stars
and our every breath a sure patient seed
climbing our spines up to their flowers of light.

PEDRO PERDIDO
— for Dean McKenzie & in memoriam Zale Martel

Sitting alone in a public privacy, you order
from someone playing at being the no-one of a slave
— but the pretence is real, realer even than the person
who won't think about pretence or freedom — a glass of wine
to be delivered to the square of legged wood you've chosen
to sit at — despite yourself, for you came here to avoid
sitting — and, after it has been handed to you in brief
bridging of two privacies extending public labels,
a scarecrow pianist, hello!, in another dark corner
of a room full of corners, starts to wave goodbye again
to a Blackbird from the edge of a firm black stool before
a stodgy varnished black piano — musical putty
to patch up this roomful of walls known as a restaurant,
the label agreed upon by those who live by God and
Webster's Dictionary for the human aquarium
of stale dusty twilit air and plastic you've plunged into —
only to feign again sitting — but it's real — and you start
to become aware through your glazed eyes' fog that the person
who delivered the wine along with a sweet yet dry smile
is bound to be something other than a prop on this stage
of your unreality, bound to be more than *Waitress*
and may be a real human, who knows — but you are cautious,
even in atoning for the shame of your blank blindness

during the long moment in which you are still pretending
to be You, a *me*, an enthroned you separate from all
other meyous, a lie your eyes defy, becoming links
between her moving about the arena of her job
— a different space from the one you have swollen into fast
like a goldfish ballooned overnight too big for its bowl —
and the tentacles of the tinkler's fingers now scuttling
in and about the murky fishtank of a tune by Monk
too well known to be announced, and its *title* is mostly
what you are now experiencing of the performer's choice
to play or replay it — *play* if you pretend it's being
played for the first time, *replay* if you fool yourself that you
are hearing one more version of *it*, something flat outside
yourself who can yet be shocked to realise the rhythms
of the woman's movements and your heartbeat, both colonised
by the score-whore's increasingly imitative fingers
— very good imitations, mind you, and these at their end
are what you'll applaud — are pulling you like a toffee-stick
in opposite directions of your urgency until
Doris/Sandra/Mary swerves around a table-corner
with a balletic spring in time to the pianist's now
frenetic pace, and this rhyming makes your heart somersault
and your sitting there worth the while, all is not *perdido*,
despite the keybored killer's already stale insistence,
not when there's such a lovely shape of rhythm now moving
towards you with a bounce in her step and wings to her hips,
not with the late sun-bow sprung off the edge of the mirror
beside your table and falling across the page of words
by which you are again trying to escape a whole world
of Table Mirror Don't Blame Meyou Thank You May I Have
Please Thank You Very Much That Was One Made Popular By.

WAITING ON THE WAITRESS

Empty hands need fire
to play with, to burn by,
so as to smoke a new

    map of the world in her tired
    face now shadowing like a cloud
    the questions of your open hand

OBSERVANT
   – for Nicole Jorgen

If innocence is impulse without lust,
it is your guileless grace that I desire.
If tenderness is a rose's cool musk,
it is the perfume of your fresh petals
that touches, angels me, a faithful cloud
that will outlive my seedings of its rain.
If caution is a flower of value,
it is the bud of your care I would keep.
If watchfulness is an eager eagle
of vulnerability on the hunt
for a chance to bridge the nearest abyss
between this need for real food and that want
of warm wine, then I long to become one
alert feather of your generous wings.

GLOW

The lantern you carry
    is your own body
of light and your beauty
    is its constant glow
at which I dare not stare
    for fear of being
shattered by its softness.

    Instead you I glimpse
out the edge of my eye
    where all miracles
remain as loose as clouds
    and are not erased
by a collector's itch
    to own them to dust.

NOTHING

            sadder than that the music be fine,
    the wine quite decent
    and the whole moment
properly nude like a newly stretched canvas
or a banquet-table waiting in moonlight
    and every stranger
    about me about
to become one more ally, and yet to find
tears thronging my eyes' gates just as they would if
    I should 'turn and see
    your fabulous face'
flashing and erasing its tales of the sun.

A MOMENT

                    is a blank ice-
rink waiting either to be
skated over or to melt.

Afraid of what these blades might
groove blind beyond erasure,
I remain at ice's edge

till you emerge like a deer
out of a forest of black
to startle me with the light

of your eyes and the caress
of the song of your silence,
promise of water somewhere

flowing and flowing and flowing

WE MEET,

                    embrace and then I can but lean
in silence towards you like a bough full
of fruits listening for the voice of the earth-
locked roots that feed it: you and I are of
the same tree of disinterested passion,
ardour well-behaved 'as a guide or mode
of hope' that will not call its name for fear
of so slackening the rope of balance taut
between not enough and too much, the path
of light above the circus-sand sprouting
dry grooved totems to the gods of routine
that promise plastic fruits and cowards' nets
of if for when (as we fear, so we must)
we fall.

WE LOVE AND THERE IS NOTHING

   to be done
about it. We didn't fall
into love but into love's
   sphere of light
you and I together
                  leapt
in order
      to live
             within
   that which none
survive without slowly cho-
   king passion.

DECISION

If I say: We may be — then *may* is
all. But if: So it is — then so we are.
And that is not mere will: I am being
dreamed through my dreams by It whose glory
is the tree of your presence in whose shade
I remain to savour the doubtless breeze
of its essence. This now can never not
be: once It is determined, It becomes
one more real dream of the mirage of Time:
true fiction, the blood of gods drawing breath.

SPEECHLESS

I love the lovely idea
she lives of herself: she is
balance embodied, that's all:
there's no more to be said.

GLIMPSE

this moth with nowhere to fly but about
the flash of your being itself circling
the moth's, drawn to its desire that mirrors
your own mirroring the moth's, this poem
with nowhere to go but towards
                                        the fresh-
rained fruit of your presence whose skin these eyes
tongue and whose juice they suckle, as at grapes
of nipples swollen with sweet rain, in sheer
greed for the other of the self, the spark
of a fruit rich with its own otherness
glistening in eyes ripe grapes that would burst
with the seeds of hope this you-and-I must
let sprout into love's new mirror of fire.

YOUR TOUCH

starts far behind the fact of your fingers
rippling like rain across the black-and-white
keys to the doors of your selves leaping out
at us like ghosts demanding recognition

and yet determined not to surrender
their enigma, even at the moment
it is revealed as no more than a mask
for containing and echoing your eyes

as decided as a kitten's paw paused
in anticipation of a moth's return;
as sharp as the claw-tip of desire's flame;
as evasive as mercury on a mirror.

43

Three:
DIVE SONG

ARRIVING AND STAYING, WATCHING

for the already-bloomed
flowers to reveal their essential
silence through their loud gestures
of colour and form determined.

BEAUTY IS NOT

an aesthetic
of limbs or masks.

The flame burns low
in a dull glass,

and statues wait
to be wakened

by the sure voice
of this other

tongue of fire.

A SCHOOLED SINGER OF STANDARDS

Squeezed notes of indecision and bluff.
Holding back, folding in: fear of not
    being correct, of being rejected
    for going too far, far outside the lines,

    the bars of the song's cage: cornered tiger.
A breather: break between voice and voice,
between silence and shape of silence:
    words carved like statues' wings, like frozen clouds
    always floating off before they can melt,
    words sentenced long before they can be felt.

WOULD MUSIC BE

    a series of moves as in a game
of football or chess that can be taught and made
with notes like words learnt and churned out with the proud
    confidence custom's cowardice sprouts

    or is music the siren fire
that precedes the sounding of the bell, waiting
at the heart of rhythm's river, listening
    for its seed's dreaming tongue, and how does

    this tongue at last utter but with leaps
like those of the salmon eager for its first
and final home and skimming the water's rush
    with flares of sheer lust for the next

    eternity when the kiss of sun,
the bite of rock and the shadow, glint and taste
of hunter's hook become one bright hosannah
    of blood sprung back to infinite light

(in memoriam Bob Stroup)

THE SONG IS YOU
  – in memoriam Ella Fitzgerald 1918-1996

Now, more than before, we know
there is no song you have not
sung: we have only to think
of one for it to become
a bell whose tongue is yours,
moreso now in the silence
of its new dangling balance.

WE LIVING

are only as bold as we entertain
    our ghosts whose presence dares sharper
than any words they tried to bequeath us.
    Yet their least song, half-remembered,
will revise itself as we continue

writing it with our every urge to sing
    ourselves: there is no escaping
the shadow of their totem of silence
    whose voice and stare, disinterested,
yet demand we sing on in the spirit

of brave flesh.

(in memoriam Noel Jeffrey Chan 1917-2007)

BEING ALONE

    is to begin
feeling the space between
    the bars of self,
between the stretched thin walls
of the puffed-out balloon
of that long-winded lie;
    is to unknot
its neck to let its stale
air escape; is to listen,
without needing to speak,
to the sigh or the scream
    of resistance
 between full and empty;
is a wordless altar
in the crowded desert
of desire for balloons
that keep bursting from get
    and from forget;
is looking away, so
as to better see,
scrawling and zigzagging
so as to chart and cross
deserts of yesterday's
totems of repeat and
    sirens of sleep.

TO BE STILL

at one point of day,
waiting for a never-before thunder again
    to throb through the vein, not habit
but masked hunt, the slack tension of a tiger perched
    in a tree of pacing nodding
monkeys and macaws, disinterested but total
    in his commitment to these limbs,
beyond any question of fall or other word,
    not even waiting but knowing
that already across the stretched scroll of air is
    drawn the arc of impulse that will
be stamped into fading rainbow when a certain
    flake of iron obeys the pull
of the magnet of focus and springs so in full
    surrender to one more exchange
between the flaming tongues of old blood and new breath

IN BETWEEN

Not a wait but
a space to keep
an idea being
born in the shape
of those to come
who may never
but always will.

BARFLY

Here I pause
to remember how not
    to sleepwalk
through trenches of custom,
    how to wake
the one essential voice
    held like wine
in cupped hands whose fingers
    lust to spread
themselves apart to shed
    their burden.

DIVE

Here I bid farewell
not to the flesh but
to its fiction out-
grown, a wine so fine
it surfeits even
as it calls for more
of itself to be
spilled in the pouring
of one more ghost glass.

ATTRACTING A BRIGHT ANGEL

                              with the hint
of a horn to a quiet song, I know
you at once, your body all wings of light
lifted by its own music's waves of sure
breathing, yet hovering
between magnets of recognition and routine,
desire and duty, ah-yes! and oh-well,
your smile a mask of baffled power,
of your admission of now-or-never,
a chance you first deny through the exit
to never, before turning back to charge
our one heart's battery, your eyes' light over-
flowing its chalice towards my hunger
to be graced by the wingtips of your breath.

YOUR SONG

                    of solitude and desire you sang
with such ardent simplicity, I felt
the smoke of your breath entwine with mine
to climb up the vine of my back, stretch
towards the raincloud of my heart
and burst it. But instead of the river
you flooded in me, what I hoped
you saw in my face's glass was the sun
of your own smile shimmering through the mist
of these eyes too overwhelmed to tell less.

STORM

Fingers of dark cloud pointed, the wind
warned, lightning threatened, but we had yet far
to lead each other by remaining
in silence's shell shaped by words of fire
the rain could not quench only echo
with its fingers drumming on the tin-roof
and slapping molten stones on the glass-walls
of our midnight sanctuary we surrendered
only to take a walk under the bones
of my old umbrella which you folded
as a mere farce after the rain nicely
refined her force to a mist and the flame
in your eyes wick'd down and gave way to smoke
in prelude to your farewell of hugging
me, afraid I might never have enough
of storms which everyone knows must pass
to allow whatever love it leaves
in its wake a chance to sprout anew

AFTER WORDS,

                         you embraced me
as though you were rescuing
a child out of the quicksand
of a floundering desire,
but who the child, whose the urge?
And did the tongue of fire fusing
your breast and mine utter not
only recognition but
also dismissal, a kind
of farewell manured by good
common sense fed by the fear
of drowning in the maelstrom
of our own insistent flames?

54

EXCHANGE

Thank you for having entertained me
  He looked as though he needed a stroke
– an old man's emotion far too base
to spine one love-poem to your youth
  so I gave him one despite myself
with the snake of fire that spirits all:
gratitude's just a pain in the ass,
  but whom was I doing a favour
a tight pout of contrast to passion's
greedy lips of generous silence.
  when my breasts sparked and peaked at his touch?

AFTERWARDS

As before:

sated   emptied   waiting

to begin

Four:
CAVE LOVE

TO MY WIFE OF TWENTY-FIVE YEARS

On our crowded cluttered path, you are my
    one elbower and hand-holder; compass and
carriage as we skirt the potholes of our mind
that keep sprouting before us with every doubt;
spirit-level and plumb of our every pause
    of reconnaissance we take at crossroads.

    We are each other's destination and
    'all the stops along the way', all the knots
of terror we tear at like foxes facing
    each other from ends of leashes made taut
    by our own tuggings as we stretch ourselves

sideways but onwards back to the ocean and
    island of our love with its temple hut
at whose midnight door I'm but the rapping wind,
    while its oven, bed, roof and raft you remain
under all clouds, throughout all thunders, after
    every flood and dove of our heart's peaked ark.

FROM THAT MOUTH TO THIS,

                                I kiss you a taste
of yourself you can never otherwise
know but by fingers, yours or mine, between
mouths. Which do you prefer? This tell-tale tongue
with its salacious gossip of your juice,
or slick imps stealing the cream of silence
to take home to the mother of babble?

But why choose? Get to know yourself every
way you can, using love's every impulse.
Only so can your innocence be re-
affirmed, on its travels between the realms
of ignorance and experience, both
openings through which the shaman of the heart
utters its oracles of shameless love.

THE KEEPER

A diffusion of shadow on a wall
beside your head bent in study: over-
lapping stages of focus: one the sharp
central dark figure of determined watch,
the second softer, from behind noting
    the fragile vanity of its leader blind
to the Thomas of yet a third conscience hovering
        below it like a failed god.

You say this reading of your shadowcast
is coloured by the clouds in my eye, scarred
by the disjunctive lines of my own face.
But it can't be only so: everything
contains a trace of all else: only see
    Picasso: what seems self-indulgent curved cubes
to Lord Larkin's blind and deadening eye is witness
        – while what can only be glimpsed

leaps to be – to each viewer's restless mind
with its angles of awareness, its shifts
of focus from hard to hazy to nought:
from everything to nothing through an I.
So I say my biases are also
    a questioning sketch of the self you can't bear
to question, lest it lead you to perceive you are not
        unicorn, but Cerberus.

BLIND

Though I know they temper your dark hell cringing
from the screaming rays of an innocent sun,
I resent these shutters pinching in the light
spreading shadows of the bars of some bright cage.

This house deserves better, fashioned as it is
of light a marriage of two heavinesses
that shoulder each other over the dark walls
dividing   desert and garden, hell and day.

JOHN DONNE TO DAME PRU

Damn it, your literalist Shit chokes,
    strangulates like a Knot of Bowels,
so don't expect I'll laugh at your Jokes
    or harmonise your pretty Vowels
        or flatter your Should
        of Good Conduct towards your Looking Good.

And when I *fuck*, don't be a Mother
    sighing at her Boy's retarded Rate
of Growth she thinks she'll fix with other
    Words that breathe less than they suffocate.
        Emotion and Mood
        let us keep as Chalices of the Good,

the Aristos of Anger, the *Cunts*
    of Passion, the *Shits* of Release, free-
breathing Speech without which Spirit wants
    to embalm the whole Shebang and be-
        come the varnished Wood
        of the long Box that shuts us up for good.

TO A TRAPPED LIONESS

Even in his sleep beside you,
your mate you can hear pacing his
rage-carpeted cage of snoring
vanity whose bars and sharp blades
of light stabbing through them are all
equally his own mind trying
to erase, and not, its tyranny
over his every breath and stamp.

Beware of feeding him your blood
and milk of your still-flowing breast.
Such food both pacifies and fills
him with despair as it keeps him
every day waking to become
his fear that his cage will, and not,
fade. Let pride to its need of Love learn
to kneel, or gnaw itself to death.

PAUSES

Our house at the heart
                          of winter's night warms itself
by blowing from its
                          heart of fire through its bones
its breath of stretches
                          snapping and crackling retorts
to the questions spun
                          of my insomniac bed
which surrenders me
                          like a hot spoon some butter

yet retains its warmth
     by the furnace of your sleep,
your temple of change
     masked as an iceberg of pause
mirrored now in my
     listening freeze on the stairs
between dark and light,
     between choosing to remain
blinded by deafness
     or awakened by the voice
of my wide-eyed dream
     burning its song through my bones.

I KNOW YOU MEAN ME

no harm when you urge me back
 home by a certain
hour, yet I feel a net drop
 about my heartbeat
before it can spark the root
 of love's tree which bears
fruit only in its own sweet
 time beyond the thorns
of the firm tree that feeds it,
 time outside the ruts
and claws of the clock's contracts.

LOVE LEFT

I:

There's a tiger gnawing
   the bloody bone of her heart screaming
   with its own hunger for the return
of a different hunter,
the arrowed angel who,
   having dined on the heart that crossed his path,
   is already many memories away
from these
       relentless teeth.

II:

Cloud-shadows are charging
   across the desert of my heart whose sands
   at every clash of winds spark and tremble
with the promise of rain.
But after the first burst
   soothes and knits the sands, a drizzle remains
   like a wall of hazy pain and the clouds
harden
     into statues.

TABLE FOR ONE – SMOKING

If a blind image-man can
   still paint what he knows,
a word-man with smudged tongue might
   yet write of his love,
a woman whose clarity,
   that knowledge before
speech, is her chief enemy
   seducing her not
to challenge its proud keep with
   speech, ally that can
help to wake a sleeper out
   of clouds of control,
days of hard moral matter
   that is only one
way of leaning on death's door.

There is always another,
   others that mirror
her other chances and so
   to their reflections
call him who has almost let
   them suck him into
their side of the looking-glass.
   Is he then as blind
to her as she missing him?
   No, he sees her most
hidden heart, the way he hears
   the voice of silence
in the detached dry report
   of a saxophone
in this room jammed with sadness.

Hers he embodies here, far
   from her, exploring
the meaning, not the allure,
   of solitude's ghost
she would prefer not to name
   or else to enter-
tain only with speech without
   any whys, leaving
no opening through which the cat
   of awe might defy
the walls and closed doors behind
   which the tree of fear
hosts the fungi of anger,
   the molds of remorse,
the cankers of hiding pride.

HOME

While you are away, I prepare
for your return by taking, out
of the cage that even the most
sacred contract could not but spore
and vein and muscle, yet one more
passage like a tongue of the sun
that leaps and dips, stretches and sucks,
draining and refilling its glass.

So I clean our house by leaving
it behind, so stamp our contract
by breaking it, and so prepare
for the return of two strangers
to the open strangeness of a cage
dismantled like a stage swept clean

in readiness for its next play
in which strangers' hearts, tongues of fire,

meet, connect and lock, unlock and let
loose, explore and find, and give away.

L'AVVENTURA DELLA NOTTE
    – *after* Antonioni

At the heart of your night, every room in the hotel
    of commitment's an empty
lobby whose swollen pillars of silence not even
    the loud mob of your desire
        to know can shift.

    The night-desk clerk is asleep
and the sharp heels of your anxiety will not wake him
    for custom's carpet never
relaxes its absorbing vigil on the chances
        of urgent pain

as it glues together your stumbles from door to door
    until you find yourself stalled
within the mouth of your chamber of revelation
    whose tongue is as stammered
        as sharp its tale,

    a grooved scrawl of your lover
betraying you with a flirt, both just coping with their
    insomniac rut more desperate
than yours for their lack of focus by dreams or through tears:
        thus you're surprised

by pity, that dicey verandah lit by the dawn
     of another forgetting
about to transform itself into Your Life with more
     demanding mountains of love
          and walls of hope.

EXPERIENCE

Into the blackest deepest cave
     the idiot goes for no other reason
than to find a way out of it,
     a way that the ragged shapeless thing alone
at the back of the cave can tell.

It is a gaunt sleep-grumbling beast
     whose clawed shaggy paw like a lost toy the gro-
ping idiot finds and embraces,
     assuming the beast is as glad to be found
and dragged into the light as he

is to become its rescuer.
     So he ignores its snarl of resistance and
its muttering of the cave's map.
     So he remains at the bottom of the cave,
his hand locked between sleeping teeth.

HAVING ACTED, I SEE

I needn't have, but I did, and that
makes the difference
between living and life,
between hoping and knowing
hope as a definite peak
in a distance only
as long as the night.

THE WAIT

HE:

     In a closed car waiting
for you who can never come back,
though you always return, I feel
    my heart shrivel

     a leaf   dry   a bone stick-
ing out of a bloodless graveyard
whose one voice is the crunch of bones
    beneath wheels deaf

     to the bells of the dead,
heeding instead only the pull
of a full moon that can't care how
    many hearts break

     themselves under her spell
and in the name of love, flinging
themselves into maelstroms of end-
    less night on earth.

SHE:

You will return always, as a leaf or a rose
after a long winter quickens to green or red.

As the sun melts the snow about my roots, I dream
my heart is a garden trembling with a new breeze

defying afternoon's slow tilt into one more
twilight of my heart's blind leap into night's spirals.

OPHELIA MAROON

Every leaf of love will return to blaze
sharp green all about me through days without
   night (and yet no star shall be
     erased). My gaze is
  the same as the sun's: neither
smile nor frown. My gown of water is all
red and white buds not yet burst like my heart.

POEM FOR DISTANT CHILDREN

A mother gives
         birth a father
can only witness,
          separated
from the fruit of his seed, his only
cord of connection (which must also
be cut) between soul and soul, mind
and mind, heart and heart (for as long
as hearts allow), all intangible
except the giving witness heart
which still moves and
           can still be touched.

POEM FOR TWO FRIENDS OF LIFE

My dear children, that I've always
been proud of you I can say now
that I've given up guarding pride
as my private silent tower.

Now I open its bells to you
as you used to share your child-strength
with a childish father who feared
bequeathing you his loneliness.

Defying my fear, you challenge
your own loneliness through your own
fears, and now, through this, with this man's
pride in his brave human comrades.

QUISÁS

I didn't know how to know you,
so I let you pass, and now you keep
crossing my path, a chilly breeze
of questions I never began
to answer or pose. Or, quisás,
that breeze is now your
                              way of saying
I didn't know how to know you.

Five:
SNOW MOON

PRESENTIMENT

A girl tells me that a boy has found
in a mirror-river a man drowned
and I don't let her know I killed him
or that the floating man is myself,

I don't even tell my own lover
for the only thought of death that she
entertains is that of melting snow,
just as the only pain she'll embrace

is birth, and she laughs and looks away
when I mention my dream of her ghost
splitting and slipping out of her life,
a blur of water through fingers slack.

JEALOUSY

In a corner drawn by two
window-walls of glass, a girl clutching
an empty jar, dry
looks over her shoulder at the rain giving

itself away to no-one
in particular, so taunting her
with a world, outside
her reach, of a careless generosity.

DOG AT YOUR DOOR

In her dark house you sisters sleep still unaware
of this barking hungry dog outside scratching hard
at the back door through which he smells your mother's ghost
burning up your bread books and boots in her oven

You wake first and shake Norma wishing she could keep
sleeping and dreaming of a song without questions
and Ruth keeps her eyes shut for she will not tell where
the key to your mother's house is that would admit

me who won't ignore her and let out you who would

ONE MORE

Love's chance, denied, its reading postponed
so that we might keep hugging our pain,
keeps returning in as many dream-
scapes as we need to finally be-
come its power, claim its glory ours.

From whisper to pinch to slap to kick,
from kick to knife to bomb to earthquake,
it keeps speaking in tongues of our masques:
Wake up wake up, your sun is dying
to be recognised as your own hearts

lest its light fade like your moment
with no one to witness its passing
but the blank fool on his midnight watch
charting falling stars throughout your sleep
of dodging your dreaded hawks of love.

TRUST

Here shine a girl and her twin who do every
thing together except bleed, so they're lovers,
each with another love, one and the same man,
a doctor who won't work weekends or airports
except to stand at their edge and wave goodbye

to both girls dressed in white, one sitting upright,
a healthy angel eager for her next cloud,
the other bent over, about to be
grounded for leaking blood and tears all over
the rugs of silence and her whites and again

she slants out of the waiting-room to the head
of a corridor and cries to the doctor
standing at its end: I need your help! — And he:
Don't you know I'm not allowed beyond this point?
Anyway, I told you: I don't do airports.

THE HABIT OF MEN

Human's a habit, a man struggling
not to become his chair stretched and ripped
like a sinew, a pirate pulling
a cutlass on the numbness
of his drunken brothers bent

on raping one another's sisters,
a monk taking hammer and chisel
to fashion gargoyles after the same
brothers who think him an ass,
a man pointing a path through

difficult mountains to his woman
who sweetly insists that they remain
on flatter ground a woman's habit,
a child pulling her balloons
behind her as she dashes

across green fields towards a cold room
in which her husband lies slabbed and tagged,
a bored queen lusting for the life-blood
of her maid about to crown
their king with flowers but reaching

instead for consolatory sweets,
a naked girl becoming the words
she reads opening her thighs to flip
through their leaves, a pallid girl
without a face who knows how

to read but has no desire to be
read, numb in her cocoon of icy
blue, a woman reading yet one more
book of herself by the light
of a man's lamp hovering

over her like a centurion,
a woman kneeling before herself,
trying to rise out of herself by
herself only to be trapped
in webs of her own spinning,

a woman about to slake her thirst
at the spring between her lover's thighs
that gives more than she would surrender,
two women putting an end
to their habit numb of men.

HABIT

The heart soars without
caring its wings must
again tire and fold
in mid-air, in mid-

A CLEVER CHILD ONCE

                        asked me, How do
people fall in love. Without
thinking, I said, out of loneliness.
Those around us laughed in embarrassed
recognition, I then thought;
now I hear them amused by my own greenness,

for now I see lovers twine their lives
together despite knowing
what knots that pregnant rope can become:
the thought of pain never deterred birth
and to live alone is too
heavy a reminder of one soul's slightness

as then there is no thing not one's own
onus, no burden lightened
by another's help, like sacks of bones
or bricks so transformed into feathers,
no moment like a sharp stone
surrendering its edges to a stream's flow.

Love, marriage and other rubbings-up
may not be more than selfish
thrusts and mocked-up shelters made to seem
inevitable, beyond question,
final like a song's coda
that tightens a noose about its root and fruit.

HEART

A cage of convenience is now my home,
a bag leaking air my bed and lying
on theirs are two women who say they miss
me whom each has given a lamp. By one
I read my heart through the life of a man
out of fashion; by the other I write
about my times by adding to their lies
my life's fictions through which but a few will
glimpse their own voice that cannot be exchanged
or refunded. So I enter one more
winter the same way a boy used to turn
a street-corner at night and find himself
walking towards dogs with flames in their eyes
and all he had between being savaged
and reaching home were his last wick of fire
held lightly between two knuckles, his eyes
of sharp fear, his feet bluffing a path through
the dogs' pause of grudging recognition
of a brother who had dared to survive
one more day of being stoned by children,
and his dark voice that could outgrowl them all.

DOG'S EYE VIEW OF THE GAME

That people move before my nose should
be enough for my type of being
that is not expected to complain
about the pointlessness of it all
especially in the cool of the day
when the sun's low enough to be light
(on my dark back heavy with stored heat).

But.   But less and less do I even care
to do But.   But's for those who can afford
to not have a leash about their neck.
The only But left me is a growl
for the idiot fooling himself
he can imagine me in my wait
(for those dark clouds to crack down at last).

DOGHOUSE

the comfort of lonely days
the taut freedom of clocklessness
the heaviness of a dense cloud
the sadness of a stretched balloon
the trembling of leaning
out of the house of the idea
of a self without having
to fall, or any lower

PAUSE

Seven then five then three black birds edged
on a blue roof bright against the evening's
rain-promising sky of slate might be

vultures shrunk by the petrol-poisoned air,
mute oracles of my dark path's text
of having to watch always the world's

casual fading of its hard focus
of spirit-numbing speed towards nothing
but cells of time paused in its collapse.

APARTMENTS

Between one loneliness of focus called *me*
and two others over there each called *tree*
dart two birds unknowing such terms
by drafting ribbons of connection between
isolations of tree and tree and these eyes
and these fingers emulating wings at play,

for what else can a winglessness hope to do
but try despite its cage of terms to be
a bird of language that might start
to reveal the web of invisible links
lacing everything together underneath
this crust of apartments built word by glazed word.

GERTRUDE BE TOKLAS

The rose is not in,
the rose is not in that
vase nor is vase holding up
rose nor is rose leaning on
vase which is not doing
rose a favour nor
versa vice.

Vase and rose contain
each other which neither
is, stretch towards and into
each other which either are,
and interwoven dance
as one, as both is,
as each are.

Though rose is vase's
and vase rose's, neither
is the other's other; rose
is vase and vase is rose and
Alice o Alice ma
semblable ma soeur, l'autre
suis un jeux.

ROSE INTO VASE

This rose you've left in my old Ukrainian vase (made
in India) sprouted only to become your gift,
as did my vase, though not to your taste, anyway
bruise itself crossing many borders in its thrust
to become yours and ours – a mongrel's lust for its
ripe moment of holding up to the light a queen
granting the world a glimpse of her brief reign of fire,

a nude flame that will keep spreading even after
she sheds her flesh of dried blood, her ghost will still grace
that Indian vase (made in the Ukraine), mine or yours
or anyone else's, it will make no difference
to the vase, whether it's lying empty or full
of earth, it will dream of the hours it was fulfilled
by our rose's perfection of determined change.

FLOWERS IN A VASE,

like children flung into an adult maze
only slowly outgrow their puzzlement
          at having been cut
          off from their mothers
whose cries of terror and loss they never
forget even as they're facing their new-
          found mortality
          of feeling what's left
of their stuttered budding slowly draining
into the water that sours to feed
          them through their last con-
          undrum of being,

becoming, and not.

84

THE SMASHED VASE

could no longer stand
the pressure of dank water
no longer feeding a blood-dry rose,
nor the doily choking the base of its stem,

    nor beside it the radio and clock
    squawking, limping, like birds hit
    by random bullets,
    nor the top

of the narrow desk
that limited its chances
to one corner of a cluttered room
whose rug could not be stained yet bristled with dust

    of dead skin devoured by dragons,
    nor the woman, blind and deaf
    to the vase's blue
    light and voice,

in tight muddy shoes
killing herself mopping up
the floor even before the vase split
and vomited its blessings all over it.

NO ETERNITIES,

      only pauses
of focus: the broken pot, buried
for centuries under tons of clay
shifting slowly between stone and dust,
dreams of one more moment of being
touched, by probing spade or careful gloves,
the moment of its next shift in time
when it starts to be something other
than what the labelling hand will claim.

 So I think of us, cracked and clogged by years
 of the weight of our mud and junk and dust,
 waiting for some flood of love to cleanse us
 but also for our moment of escape
 from the very fingers of rain that would
 unclog us from the burden of ourselves,
 the comforting pain we won't surrender,
 instead choosing to slip out of love's hold
 to fall and smash into another shape
 of beautiful interesting hell on earth.

A MOTH DOUBLED

                              itself on my mirror
and so came between my two faces.
I smothered it between my fingers

    covered with paper as soft as its wings:
    surprising things are best killed
    with the most care, the least mess:
    suffocate them with kindness.

And of course there are necessary crimes
like cutting down grass you ask to grow
and poisoning food to keep it *fresh*.

    In this case there were curtains to protect.
    But in truth I killed the moth
    because I could: such evil
    is reflexive, commonplace,

and the maudlin murderer in me thanks
this murderee for its gift of death,
its message of flesh's impotence

    in the face of our density of masks
    and their demanding habits
    that deaden as they comfort
    and keep our mirrors blinding.

CONFIRMATION

In a moment of idleness I draw
a sunflower of perfect simplicity
out of the giving morning-air that you
can not perceive behind your sleeping eye.

This flower then is no-one's if not mine
— although nothing of mine belongs to me —
a gift of the light that will keep on shining
whether or not there's someone here to see it

— my child-knowledge your blind wisdom returns me,
making of a bud-boy a day's-eye-man
who'll give the flower whenever he can
while holding the sun even as it burns him.

Six:
FIRE WIND

SUMMER MORNING MOUNTAIN

A casual cloud robs the sun
of its naked knives that melt
off the surface of this rock
and drain the day of its ghosts

so that trees stand unerased
into a darker denser green
that sharpen them to moreso
actual and so more strange.

A STRAY

        wisp of cloud
                drifted
up from behind a mountain, crumbled
and dissolved. Was I the only witness
of its determined self-erasing course?
The mountain sighs: Of course not;
nor was it an omen of only your
death: ask that crow in flight
and he will tell you: We are all
drifting in and out of being:
ask that mountain ever reaching
for the nudity by which it keeps redefining its focus
of nakedness, while we, bird and cloud
and man, by contrast of our faster fading,
lend it an illusion of fixity, feed
its dream of timeless solidness whose value
as eternal witness of our cloudiness we invent.

INTEREST

A stain on a map lures one wheeled crate after another
    to this Point of Interest where they pause to allow
tourists bundled together (but in separate seats, of course)
    to step down, stretch their legs, smoke, look around and take
photographs (those without cameras pocket or fold their hands)
    of one another posed against this mountain or
that hotel or beside that sign that tells them what to see,
    and it's all more demanding evidence that they
exist, future proof that each life won't have been without its
    points of interest. What can such solipsism have
to do with vision or vision to do with collecting
    butterflies flattened under glass and calling that
experience? Is the unreal all that we know how to live?
    Don't we all just pays our cash and takes what we gets?
What makes *this* telling lie any different, what grand intent?
    What difference can intent or vision make, any?
(My questions are mirrored in one child's frowning puzzlement
    as she reboards her bus headed for the next stain.)

TWO POEMS FOR TERENCE ROBERTS

I: ROCKS OFF A HIGHWAY IN ONTARIO

These broken teeth of time's dreaming
walls grimace with but a hint
of poverty their staggered history
of ruthless human blades and blasts.

II: TWILIGHT OVER SASKATOON

Out of the blue-jade
   gouache of a smoky sky,
      the perfect batik-dot of a sun
        stares de haut en bas at us riding this bus
     as though neither it nor we must fade,
   nor the earth turn nor the eye
more gradually dark.

TWO POEMS FOR MILTON DREPAUL

I: FULL MOON OVER NIGHTBUS

Not even such a decided
moon views us from only one side
and even if we chose
            to stay
still her angle would keep
             shifting
until she could no more afford
to spare us the light in her eye
or we lost her behind the blind
tears of another yawning dawn.

II: THE WEALTH OF A WAIF

Some generous cloud of a bird left us
a tip on the sky's table, a feather
of light that, even though it's nothing but
a gesture of the full thing, we call Moon,
thinking we know there's more where that comes from.

IN THE GARDEN

    The lives of plants are only
    as secret as we are blind

to their masks, as dumb as we are deaf
to the crackling silence of their tongues.

    To these this stray ladybird
    has no trouble responding

with her casual but thorough caress
that leaves unadored no pore of this

    geranium's flesh of fire
    to make it, more brazen, blaze.

THE CANADIAN OCTOBER TREE

in this lobby knows
no season but a standardised summer
to oblige with greenish branches. Only
a few leaves puzzled
by the tree's seed-memory of autumn
have drained their colour. A few others, less
unsure (more faithful),

have already leapt
down into their new status of rug-stain.
But the tree, a mother by now resigned
to her solitude
of an eternity in soil without
depth, stands well-clad still, saving nature's face,
if not her full fire.

THERE'S A THREE-LEGGED DOG

keeping pace with his brisk unsentimental mistress
who leads him across
pulsing veins of impatience we call city-traffic
and makes him climb stairs.
All this he does with a graceful lack of fuss: nothing
to do but balance
from the centre of his lack of symmetry, the line
quivering between
his eye and the ground his second fourth and first fifth leg.

HINT

Fallen leaves that lead back to a tree also
extend from it, as much as do full branches,
as issues of the map of its utterance,
the way the stars that seem random are balanced
by a centre whose nature it is to keep
dividing itself into more and more points
of light so that we shall uncover never
any absolute but the hint of its winks.

DESIRE MILES AWAY HERE

The scope of unruffled green that sucked me in
is now a million blades of bright disinterest
which allow the wind to fondle them as you
don't mind my combing my fingers through your hair
although you'd hardly miss it if I didn't.

In walking into my picture I am drawn
into its erasure become another
image in which you a mile away might
                                        start
to glimpse something other
                                    than the wind passing
through a lovely detachment of calling green.

THE WIND AGAIN

erases any cloud
of hope left us and I let
bombs and candles flicker
and your coffee cold stagnate.

All night I hold vigil
with apples and sunflowers
in their bowl and vase, still
screaming for their cut mothers.

Livelier than their form are
their shadows: memory and
conscience sprout of the same
earth, and although one appears

to survive a dry bowl
and the other dank water,
both must kneel to the wind
which nothing withstands, nothing.

WORK

The busyness of others
alarms me, and yet (and so)
on my own, busy do I
become, moving towards my
next appointment of desire,

unlike trees in a windstorm
flailing their limbs beyond hope,
beyond want of anything
but the pleasure of the dance
as its service to the wind.

Or: seeing others rushing
to execute some excuse
for coming together known
as Work, I sigh and lean back,
witness to those fallen leaves

which, once they pretend to be
dead, can leap up when the wind
moves them beyond all effort,
nothing to do but dance
the Wind-way that Work forgets.

SUN WIND

Waiting for the sun, I witness the wind.
This is what she does: she allows the grass
to fool itself it can run; she lets trees
pretend they have wings to stretch and feathers to spare;

she pushes against boys biking to school;
she helps along girls wearing awkward shoes
but shows no respect for their skirts or hair;
she sends hats and trashcan-lids rolling down the street.

The wind can drive men mad, if they resent
or resist her, fearing she'll blow away
their plans or ideals, blow open their plots,
their secrets or their other unspoken notions.

Tornado winds have erased entire towns
and those who don't die learn anew to thank
the Lord and praise Him for His sublime works.
I have always entertained the wind: we've been friends

ever since she gave me hell in the rain
as I towed my children on my bike, bags
of food on my shoulders, one hand steering,
the other steadying an open umbrella.

We go back, the wind and I, and she'll still
use my ears as doorways into my head
where she clears away any cobwebs and
leaves behind her echoes to haunt me: she likes me:

once in the grass she was about to cross
paths with me when she changed her mind and rushed
towards me and kissed me like no woman
ever has, like a big friendly dog or a child.

There's also 'solar wind' — which reminds me
that what I've been waiting for has arrived
on my shoulder perched like a bird there blown
by the wind whom, through these thoughts of her, I become.

MY LAST ONE

The wind offers to relieve me
of my habits and other drugs if
my mind I let her feather.

Other, commonsensical folk
see it this way: 'There's a storm comin','
and close their windows and doors.

I leave cracks in mine, to let in
the wind that blows my papers about,
making me dash to save these

always being born: these I think
I'll keep — as though my whole bay would crash
if I let go but one leaf

that anyhow belongs to her
who signed it but for a few to read.
My last drug's the wind herself.

ABOUT THE AUTHOR

Brian Chan was born in Guyana in 1949. He began to establish a reputation as a poet of talent with his work in *Expression* in the early 1970s, part of a group that included Janice Lowe (Shinebourne) and N.D. Williams. He had poems published in *Caribbean Quarterly, Artrage*, and *One People's Grief* and is included in the Heinemann anthology of Caribbean poetry.

His first collection of poems, *Thief With Leaf* (1988) won the 1988 Guyana Prize. His work is challenging and experimental, exploring not only experience, but the fictions we create in making sense of experience. He moved to Canada in the 1970s and his poems explore a territory in which Guyanese memories filter into the Canadian present. He currently lives in Edmonton. His second collection of poems, *Fabula Rasa*, was published in 1994.

He is a musician (clarinetist) and accomplished painter.

ALSO BY BRIAN CHAN

Brian Chan
Thief With Leaf
ISBN: 9780948833229; pp. 56; 1988, £7.99

Jan Shinebourne writes: 'The distinguishing mark of Brian Chan's poems is that they constantly illuminate the moments of everyday living; wherever the poet finds himself, glimpses of actual and remembered scenes come to him in moving detail... Each poem in this selection is life-enhancing. There is no vain pursuit or striving after slogans, catchphrases, sentiment, or any other seductive, transient passions. For the poet, poetry at its best is like a best friend, trustworthy and of lasting value, an art in which to invest an individual's own quest for permanence, an art through which to converse sincerely, explore and transcend experiences, so we find in them a voice which expresses the most permanent qualities of vision. This is a collection of poems essentially of spiritual questing, Zen-like, giving at their best a quiet spiritual aura to the everyday.'

Brian Chan
Fabula Rasa
ISBN: 9780948833595; pp. 118, 1994, £8.99

Brian Chan's poetry goes beyond everyday appearance to the inner space where the consciousness 'begins to question the power of space it has fictioned'. In staring into the abyss over which such fictions are spun, *Fabula Rasa* challenges all comfortable and solid assumptions. Thus, those poems which affirm the power of love or celebrate those moments 'brimming with light', seem both more powerful and more movingly vulnerable in their act of affirmation. Chan's poetry requires close attention but has a pellucid quality: 'Plumbing my darkest heart, I shape the glass/ of plain mind in which you may taste your own'.

TITLES BY OTHER MEMBERS OF THE EXPRESSION GROUP

Jan Lowe Shinebourne
Timepiece
ISBN: 9780948833038; pp. 186; 1986; £8.99

Sandra Yansen must leave behind the ties of family and her Berbice village when she takes up a job as a reporter in Georgetown. When she says goodbye to her friends she feels that she is betraying them. She finds the capital riven by racial conflict and the growing subversion of political freedom. Her newspaper has become the mouthpiece of the ruling party and she finds her ability to tell the truth increasingly restricted, whilst in the office she has to confront the chauvinism and vulnerability of her male colleagues.

Yet, uncomfortable as she frequently is, Sandra knows that she is growing in a way that Pheasant would not allow. But when her mother's illness summons her home, and she re-encounters the matriarchy of Nurse, Miss K.and Noor, she knows again how much she is losing. It is their values that must sustain her search for an independence which does not betray Pheasant's communal strengths.

Jan Lowe Shinebourne
The Last English Plantation
ISBN: 9781900715331; pp. 182; 1988; £8.99

'So you want to be a coolie woman?' This accusation thrown at twelve year old June Lehall by her mother signifies only one of the crises June faces during the two dramatic weeks this novel describes. June has to confront her mixed Indian-Chinese background in a situation of heightened racial tensions, the loss of her former friends when she wins a scholarship to the local high school, the upheaval of the industrial struggle on the sugar estate where she lives, and the arrival of British troops as Guyana explodes into political turmoil.

Merle Collins writes: '...Her achievement lies in having the voices of the New Dam villagers dominate the politically turbulent period of 1950s Guyana – a wonderful and stimulating voyage into the lives behind the headlines, into the past that continues creating the changing present...'

Jan Lowe Shinebourne
The Godmother and other Stories
ISBN: 9781900715874; pp. 160; 2004; £7.99

Covering more than four decades in the lives of Guyanese at home or in exile, these stories focus on characters at points of crisis. Harold is celebrating the victory of the political party he supports whilst confronting a sense of his own powerlessness; Chuni is confused by the climate of revolutionary sloganizing which masks the true situation: the rise of a new middle class, elevated by their loyalty to the ruling party. This class, as the maid, Vera, recognises, are simply the old masters with new Black faces.

Other stories echo the experience of many thousands who fled from the political repression, corruption and social collapse of the 70s and 80s. The awareness of the characters is shot through with Guyanese images, voices and unanswered questions. It is through these that their new experiences of Britain and North America are filtered.

N.D. Williams
The Crying of Rainbirds
ISBN: 9780948833403; pp. 162;1991; £8.99

Torn between despair over 'the rancid taste of life on the island' and attachment to the 'irresistible, green island days', the characters in these short stories inhabit a Caribbean they find it impossible to live in, yet impossible to live without. They dream of being inviolable and whole, but live in situations which are frequently on the edge of disorder and personal threat. Yet there is nothing wearily pessimistic about the tone of this collection. Williams's stories, like his characters, are intensely alive. Their individual voices button-hole us and won't let us go. Their tales are sad, but what passion they have in their pursuit of meaning!

N.D. Williams
The Silence of Islands
ISBN: 9780948833465; pp. 196; 1994; £8.99

Delia Mohammed gives Mr. Ni Win two bags for safe keeping. In them he finds her story of escape from the suffocations of her father and Caribbean island life into the nightmarish world of an illegal immigrant in America. Abandoned at customs by her lover, Trinidad, who turns out to be not at all what he seems, Delia is forced to fend for herself. She brings to the task both an acute intelligence and a naievety born of her greater familiarity with literature than with life. But if literature is no guide to the hazards of migrant life, it provides Delia with meaning and psychic protection, and the resonances, with *King Lear*, for instance, give the novel a wholly convincing depth.

N.D. Williams
Prash and Ras
ISBN: 9781900715003; pp. 192; 1997; £8.99

Disparate worlds collide in Williams's two novellas. In 'My Planet of Ras' a young German woman joins a Rastafarian commune in Jamaica. Under their guidance she learns to marvel, and to understand the true nature of community. Williams' portrayal of the rootedness, the inner calm and visionary enlightment of the group is movingly convincing, not least because he realistically conveys the group's vulnerability, temptations and the costs of their denials. In their rejection of materialism and competition, they indeed have to live as if they are on another planet, constantly threatened by the surrounding Babylon.

'What Happening There, Prash', is a contrary and equally convincing portrayal of the magnetic pull of North America and its offer of the possibilities of individual recognition and material success. Prash and his wife Sookmoon abandon the decaying 'socialist' republic of Guyana for New York and for Sookmoon, at least, there is the chance, eagerly seized, to remake her life as a liberated woman. But when Prash gets mixed up in some serious drugs business, he discovers that the freedom of the market has its price.

N.D. Williams
Julie Mango
ISBN: 9781900715775; pp. 300; 2004; £9.99

Williams' characters are invariably in motion or grappling with its temptations. They are returning to the Caribbean after long absences abroad, on the verge of leaving to make new lives or struggling to contain the frustrations of island life within their decisions to stay put. Though several of the stories focus on the pretensions of 'The Republic' (Guyana in its most self-consciously socialist imposture), Williams' stage is the wider Caribbean diaspora, in the UK, Brooklyn or Toronto: the Caribbean that never leaves his characters' heads.

His characters' are anxious not to be swept away into the anonymous mass, though this stance is not unproblematic: the narrator of 'Batty Bwoy, Divert', for instance, has to deal with the contradictions between his attractions to Rastafarianism and his discomfort, as a gay man, over Rasta homophobia. What Williams's characters want is the space to cultivate their sense of individual worth, though this can sometimes involve becoming trapped in an absurd or confining persona. At the heart of all the stories is the plea for a humane tolerance.

All titles available online at www.peepaltreepress.com
or enquire at contact@peepaltreepress.com